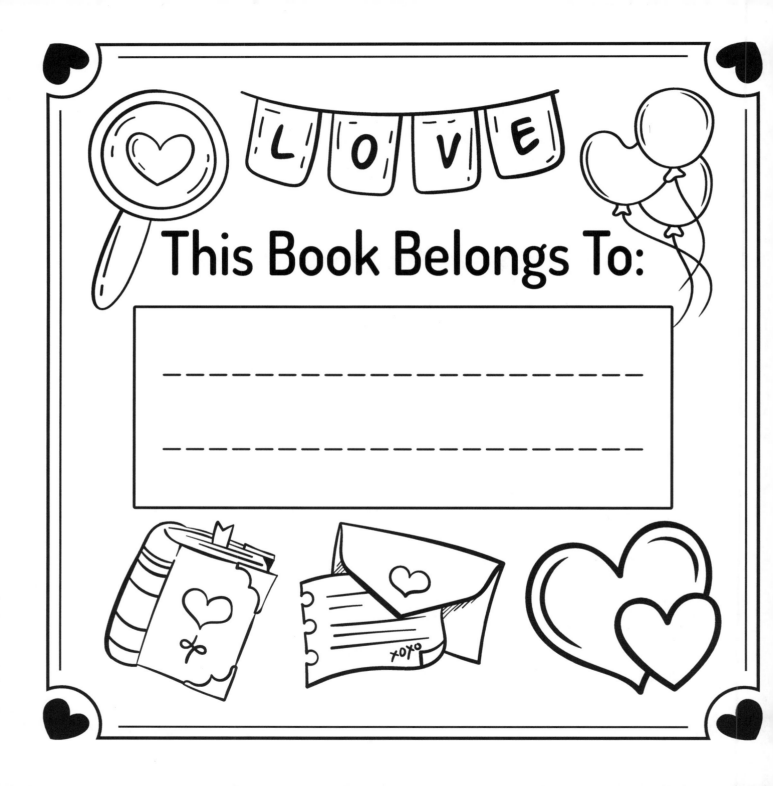

LOVE

This Book Belongs To:

_____

_____

I Spy with my little eye
Something beginning with ...

Arrows

I Spy with my little eye
Something beginning with ...

B

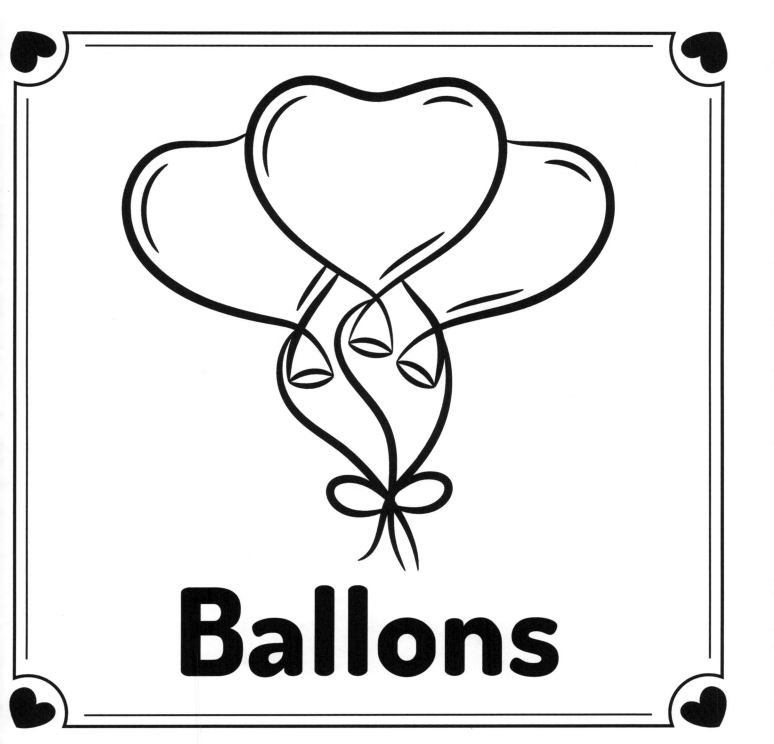

Ballons

I Spy with my little eye
Something beginning with ...

Cupid

I Spy with my little eye Something beginning with ...

D

Doves

I Spy with my little eye
Something beginning with ...

Envelope

I Spy with my little eye
Something beginning with ...

Flowers bokeh

I Spy with my little eye
Something beginning with ...

Gift box

I Spy with my little eye
Something beginning with ...

Hearts

I Spy with my little eye
Something beginning with ...

Imp

I Spy with my little eye Something beginning with ...

Jar

I Spy with my little eye
Something beginning with ...

Kangaroo

I Spy with my little eye
Something beginning with ...

Love Book

I Spy with my little eye
Something beginning with ...

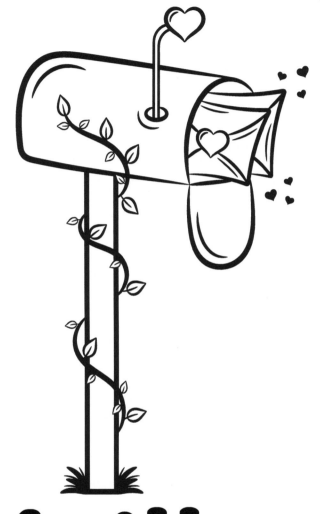

Mailbox

I Spy with my little eye Something beginning with ...

Narwhal

I Spy with my little eye Something beginning with ...

Owl

I Spy with my little eye
Something beginning with ...

Potion

I Spy with my little eye Something beginning with ...

Queen

I Spy with my little eye
Something beginning with ...

R

Rose

I Spy with my little eye
Something beginning with ...

Sweetheart calendar

I Spy with my little eye Something beginning with ...

Teddy bear

I Spy with my little eye
Something beginning with ...

Unicorn

I Spy with my little eye
Something beginning with ...

Violin

I Spy with my little eye Something beginning with ...

Whale

I Spy with my little eye
Something beginning with ...

I Spy with my little eye Something beginning with ...

Yogurt

I Spy with my little eye
Something beginning with ...

Zeppelin

I hope you enjoyed
Leave us a feedback!
it's gone be helpfull to make
good books for your child

Made in the USA
Middletown, DE
13 January 2023

22115489R00060